Lord Keep Me Motivated

REGINALD C. ROSE II.

Thirteen13Publishing

LORD KEEP ME MOTIVATED

CONTENTS

"LORD KEEP ME MOTIVATED"

FORWARD

This book I dedicate to my wife Crystal and my children Reginald and Heaven. Thanks for the love and support you have given. And thanks for being patient with me as I took you on a roller coaster of emotions over the last few years. I am thankful for the hugs and hangouts I needed through this process. I am grateful to God for you and I love you very much.

I want to thank my parents and family for providing me with the spiritual foundation. Thanks for the love and support you have given me over the years. Thank you for every kind word, the constant wisdom, and the inspiration you've given me to continue to pursue my calling even in difficult times. And finally, I would like to thank God for allowing me to lead the Mt. Paran Church, which has reshaped my life and idea of ministry. Thank you for all the love, support, and push to be the best for God.

My main reason for this writing stemmed from my conviction of perfection in Christianity and its deception. While the Lord calls us into a life of *"holiness,"* it is not our clothes or words that make us perfect. Perfection is Christ in us and his work that gives us a *"complete"* or *"fully furnished life."*

Too often, a façade is up in many believers' lives. They appear to be one thing in the eyes of others, but they do not realize that God sees them for who they are. And guess what? I had started being one of them! I could preach and teach about joy, discipline, obedience, motivation, and inspiration, but there were years I wasn't living it in reality.

My prayer for those who read these pages is for the Lord to give you the same motivation that he was able to provide for me during one of the most trying seasons of my life. It will take dedication and focus to complete, but I promise the journey will plant a seed that God will continually water. And in the years to come, you will be able to see His fruit in your life.

"HOW TO USE THIS BOOK"

This book's aim is to motivate the reader to be committed to God even amidst the vicissitudes that life presents. To maximize the effectiveness of the material, here are a few tips to incorporate into your Bible study and devotional time with God.

1. Set out a specific time of about 20-25 min for reading and meditation. Read the Biblical text first before you read the lesson material. This process will ensure you have a general understanding of the material.
2. There is a section for notes to help you brainstorm, write down your thoughts from the reading, or write your prayers and any other ideas God gives you in your studies.
3. Finally, stay committed to the schedule. This study aims to help the reader do two things: (1) Practice discipline and (2) Stay motivated on your Christian journey.

My prayer for you is that through this study, you will be able to identify similarities between the characters and be inspired to know that God is always with you. And when you must go through the tough times of life, remember with the help of the Lord, you will remain Motivated!

INTRODUCTION

Where did this topic, *"Lord Keep Me Motivated"* come from? This topic evolved from my struggles as a man, Pastor, husband, father, child, sibling, and friend to remain motivated as a Christian. I began a journey reading various authors on topics like prayer, joy, surrendering of self, and finding peace, which for a short moment seemed to work. But as time would reveal, motivation was short-lived because it only placed a band-aid over a deep womb that had become infected from the years of neglect in my spiritual development.

I often struggle with the notion, *"I am a Christian, but why are there times when I simply did not feel like one?"* One day, the light finally came on. I was taking a course in seminary on personal spiritual development when I read a book entitled, "*The Emotionally Healthy Church.*" Initially, I thought it was a topic on how the congregation needed to mature for the church to be healthy.

But as I read, I discovered it was not about membership deficiencies, it exposed my weaknesses and struggles. From the opening pages, the author's testimony was like I was staring in the mirror. He described several ways he and others allowed their issues to get put on the back burner while they attempted to be firemen in other's problems. I discovered that was where I was.

In this study, I was to perform a history test on my own life. And it was through this test I uncovered some hurtful situations I suppressed from my past. What I discovered was shocking. I was guilty of being a workaholic but neglected my personal development in God.

After performing the evaluation and reading the scriptures, I can say that exposing my weakness did not feel great. It was totally out of my comfort zone, but it proved to be what I needed to engage in a meaningful devotional study of God's word.

I grew up in a culture where hardship, social injustice, and racial discrimination have destroyed men's ability to show emotion. Naturally, men will demonstrate only a few emotions, fear, anger, jealousy, and rage. At an early age, I learned crying was for wimps. And the standard in our culture was, *"No wimps allowed!"*

In our family, I never saw my father or grandfather cry. If there was something I deemed traumatic and I wanted to cry, I heard the words, *"Suck it up! Because big boys don't cry!"* This motto became my reality for decades. So, I never cried or showed any emotion outwardly. I appeared to be intact, but my inner man was suffering.

I found myself in a hard place. I had to see a specialist for migraine headaches, low blood pressure, and depression. I came to identify all these things were happening because I did not allow myself to be vulnerable to my feelings, and I hid them and hurt myself in the process.

In 2020, I lost two of my grandmothers about 28 days apart. I found myself adopting the emotional training system I had learned from my past. I did not cry or show any emotion on the outside. I proclaimed God's word on both occasions. The people who heard the sermons testified it blessed them. On the outside, I was cool, but inside I was weeping. I felt that if I took time to grieve myself, where would others in my family get their strength from?

It is funny to write that last statement because I've preached Psalm 46 which says, *"God is our refuge and strength a very present help in times of trouble."* And there I was, trying to be something for others that only God could be for them. I did not realize that when I embrace grief, it is a way that I can be more like God.

So, I took the David journey and discovered that while he wrote Psalms of praise, he also wrote Psalms of lament. These two spectrums of emotions clarify that it is okay to feel, cry, grieve, and mourn. I have now planned to meditate and accept the truth of scripture. I am learning from David that when others hurt you, there is no need to suppress how you feel, but you can tell God and rely on him being the strength you need to *"keep you motivated!"*

Have you ever found yourself where it was hard to find motivation? I discovered that the standards I witnessed in Christianity did not equate to the life God purposed me to live. I had seen how many would live by the code, *"You can have your cake and eat it too."* This principle taught that because God forgives, you can do whatever pleases you. But then I was reminded by Paul in Romans 6:1-2 *"What shall we say then? Are we to continue in sin that grace may abound? By no means! How can we who died to sin still live in it?"* [1]

I finally discovered my issue. I was guilty of living in sin. This discovery is when I begin a journey for God to deliver and develop me. I wanted to live according to the standards that would please God. It had to be practical and keep me motivated, no matter what.

One of the key figures in the Bible who inspired me was the Apostle Paul. In the book of Colossians, he voiced where the source of motivation starts. Paul was suffering, yet he was rejoicing. He realized what I needed to realize, which was, that we are only stewards of the grace of God. This stewardship means we have a responsibility to share the word of God. In his final words, he gave me the motivation I needed to begin my journey and I pray his words will help you to remain motivated.

"Him we proclaim, warning everyone and teaching everyone, that we may present everyone mature in Christ. For this I toil, struggling with all His energy that He powerfully works within me." (Colossians 1:28-29 ESV) [2]

The keywords that inspired and helped me is when Paul highlighted that *"in everything he did it is not because of him."* This power comes from God's energy and His power working in us. Let these words of Paul also help be the launching pad into a life of joyful, motivated service to the Lord despite the difficulties. As you read these pages, you will notice a constant cry to God, in addition to inspiration gleaned from each passage of the Bible. May these expressions give you hope and motivation for the future.

| 1 |

"Lord keep me motivated when I'm worrying about things I cannot control."

Read: Philippians 4:6-7 and Matthew 6:25-34

Why do we worry? And how does worrying affect our lives? As humans we have a tendency to consume ourselves with worry. For example, we worry about our health, finances, relationships, and as I like to call the *"What ifs of life."*

Barbra Johnson a well know Christian author said it best, *"Worrying is the senseless process of cluttering up tomorrow's opportunities, with leftover problems of today."* [3]

And if the truth be told, people spend more time worrying than we spend on doing anything else. We worry about the possibilities and impossibilities of life. We worry about our families, friends, and our shortcomings. I once heard someone say in a message, *"We worry about the past, we cannot change, we worry about things that may happen in the future, which we have no control over, and we worry about the possibility of things happening, which is simply a waste of time."*

Therefore, we clutter up our lives, not understanding God has already given us a system that will help us to stay clutter-free and maximize the opportunities he provides. What would happen in our lives if we worried less? And is it possible to not worry? The answer is yes! So, why do we worry?
I have discovered too often people live lives filled with worry because of the lack of communication and reliance on God. I am guilty of this, and guess what so are you. The final question is, "What does the Bible teach us about worrying?

Here is a simple way to put it....... **Don't Do It!** Jesus said it like this, *"Therefore I tell you, do not be anxious about your life, what you will eat or what you will drink, nor about your body, what you will put on. Is not life more than food, and the body more than clothing? (Matthew 6:25)* [4]

Unfortunately, when life falls apart, we do too, and if we will be transparent when we are at our weakest, that is when we should seek the Lord most, but in actuality, it is when we seek him the least. Why? Because we become blinded by our feelings, and in pride, we try to fix things that only God can solder back together. This is why Paul gives us these encouraging words to help us receive the mending our hearts desperately need. Paul in essence tells us to pray more and worry less, but how?

Here is the fourfold remedy we need from the text......

Don't Be Anxious for Anything (6)

We need to know that the Lord is always available to us. We all must understand there are particulars about the world and life we do not understand and will probably never understand. These are the elements that I like to call the *"certain uncertainties."* These are *"certainties"* about life that we do not understand because of the *"uncertainty"* of its timing, but the key is we must not worry about it.

Why? Because we serve a God that is available to us at all times. Therefore, when we find ourselves unmotivated to serve God and to live for him, the first thing we need to do is, stop and follow Paul's instruction to *"not"* be anxious for or about *"anything"* but in *"everything* we must learn to be prayerful in *"everything."*

Be Prayerful in Everything (6)

We must know when we are trying to understand how *"not"* to worry about *"anything,"* the key is to know that the Lord is always accessible to us. One songwriter said. *"I can call him in the morning, I can call him in the middle of the night, and when I call him, he will make everything all right. Jesus promised he'll take care of me"* [5]

The *"calling on him"* is called prayer. When Paul uses the terms prayer and supplications, he is helping us understand that when we feel helpless, we can plead to God with a sense of urgency about our situation. The problem that many do not consider is every time we take a breath in this fallen, sinful world, it is a blessing we have not been consumed.

So, every morning the Lord wakes us, we should earnestly seek the Lord to protect us, guide us, and lead us in paths of righteousness amidst our unrighteous society. God has given us prayer as the avenue of communication. And all we have to do is call on him and he will answer. Next, Paul tells us that we must learn to be thankful unto God for everything he has provided.

Be Thankful for Everything (6)

As we all know, through the ebbs and flows of life, there have been instances that should have taken us out, but the fact remains that we are still here! And because we are still here, it is a constant reminder that God is worthy of all our thanks. Therefore, anything the Lord gives us is a reason for us to give thanks.

Just in case someone reading these pages has forgotten what God has done, here is a practical list of reminders. (1) It is the Lord who woke you up. (2) It is the Lord who kept you from losing your mind. (3) It is the Lord who provides for your family. (4) It is the Lord who purchased you off the slave market of sin. (5) It was the Lord who laid down his life for sinners like you and I. (6) It is that Lord who has been, who will be, and who is always on our side. We who are his children need to learn that we should give him thanks for anything and everything he has provided. Paul concludes our study by sharing that we can have peace in everything.

Have Peace in Everything (7)

Finally, we can rejoice because *"the Lord is always alert"* to what we need and when we need it. The Bible says he does not slumber nor does he sleep. The Lord is always where he has been and He will be where he has always been! In other words, you can depend on God. There is one condition. God is only there for those who know him and have trusted him for salvation. So, when you know who God is, you can have peace in your circumstances because you understand God is the only one who can provide it.

Man's biggest problem is we are guilty of trying to get peace in the wrong places, people, and things. The good news is the only one who can give us peace is God. We will never escape troubles and tribulation on this side of heaven, so while we are here, we must know that we have access to God, who will give us his peace. God's peace supersedes our understanding, and it guards our hearts, which are our thoughts, feelings, and emotions. God's peace also guards our minds.

This is important because it is how we reason. The reality is when you are in Christ, God gives us the ability to have peace about, in, and through all things, but we must keep our minds focused on him. Therefore, when those times of anxiety try to rear its ugly head and attempt to command our attention, remember you have a relationship with the Almighty God.

So, cast all your cares upon him because he cares for you. When we learn to give all our cares to him, nothing will make us anxious, and we will remain motivated. How will we know when it happens? Everything will cause us to pray. And with everything we have, we will be thankful because we serve a God who will give us peace in all things. Therefore, we must learn to *"pray more, and worry less."*

Prayer:

Dear Lord, help me depend on you when I do not know what to do next. I have been guilty of attempting to solve my issues apart from you. I ask for you to forgive me and give me a heart to trust in you. Thank you for providing for me and giving me the greatest gift of salvation through your Son. Lord, help me to depend on you more and rely on myself less. In Jesus' Name Amen.

LORD KEEP ME MOTIVATED

Notes

____

____

____

____

____

____

____

____

____

____

____

____

____

____

____

____

| 2 |

"Lord keep me motivated to develop as you have purposed."

Read: Genesis 12:1-20

Today, we live in an instant society where no one is willing to be patient and wait on anything. When we go to restaurants and order our food, how and when do we want it? Of course, we want it instantly. And why? Because we are impatient. It is sad, but the truth is people want everything to happen as quickly as they think of it.

But what happens when God says we must wait? What happened to being patient while you are going through the development process? I have discovered that the moments I get too impatient waiting on God is also the moment I lose motivation. But through trials and temptations, I have learned that waiting on God and trusting him will pay off in the end.

Remember back in the day, we used to buy disposable cameras to take pictures. We had to take the cameras to a Walgreens or local drug store to develop the photos. The development process was that you would not be able to see and appreciate the photos you had taken until the process was completed. And I believe that many of us have gotten too used to an *"instantaneous mindset"* and now it is hard for us to go through the process of growing and developing.

In the same way, the pictures needed to go through the development process, so do we. Because the photo of our lives must come out the way God planned it. Many live smeared lives because we don't want to go through the process.

In the text, we find a man who knew something about having to go through a process. He had received a promise, but to receive the promise he had to go through the process first, and why?

Because going through the process *"develops character."* Abram and his family have moved from Ur, going to Canaan. But when they arrived in Haran, they settled there instead. Abram's father died in Haran, and it was there where Abram heard from the Lord to leave everything and relocate to where God would send him. What did Abram do? Abram heard, and he responded to God.

This action is just the opposite for most people because what people do when they receive directions they are unfamiliar with they stop, before they start. But why? The issue is not that they have not heard the instructions. The problem is they have decided not to accept the instructions from God. This reaction happens because people would rather not take on any added pressures, difficulties, or adversities in their lives, which are vital in the development process.

The Bible teaches no temptation can put a hold on us because temptations are a common element to man. This teaching means there are no new situations, problems, or hurts to experience. Everyone will experience these elements at one time or another.

The issue most people have is they don't want to go through the process because they want to receive what can only come through a process. But what did Abram do? He acts upon the instructions he received from the Lord without asking questions and without knowing what he would have to endure along the way.

Abram does something imperative before he moves in the direction God instructed. He *"prepares"* himself and his family before they begin their journey. Even though Abram receives the instructions and begins to move, there is a process he has to go through to *"develop the character"* in him that God requires.

In the text, one major character flaw existed in Abram that needed to be corrected, which was telling *"lies."* Abram, like many of us, will do things naturally to protect ourselves and not trust God.

What do you do when times of famine come in your life? When everything is out of your control? When it feels like there is no hope? And how do you begin to think in those times of famine? All of these questions must be considered because we are not much different than Abram.

Notice how Abram handled the situation, he looked at the situation instead of looking to His God. Does that sound like you? No situation will arise in life that is greater or more powerful than God. Abram, like many people today, has made a rash decision without seeking God. For instance, when we strive after our spouse, a career, a business opportunity, church, or any other aspect, we are quick to seek counsel from others, and we neglect to seek God, who made and sustains all life.

The question is why? Could it be that we think that our issues are too great for God? Instead of asking God, Abram relied on human intuition, and he *"lied"* when the heat turned up. God didn't leave Abram to think that what he was doing was okay; he showed him that what God says and where God sends, he doesn't need our assistance to sustain.

In other words, God does not need our help. This truth should reassure us that just as God allowed Abram to gain even in famine, he can motivate us in any hard place we find ourselves in. It was God who punished Pharaoh and set Abram free, and it was God who gave Abram more than what he had when he went in.

The key to understanding this truth is Abram had to go through the process before he could understand as long as God is with him, everything will work out for his good. The same is true for the believer, we also must remember God is with us, and everything will work out for our good.

Prayer:

Lord, I know there are still areas in my life where I need development. Forgive me for trying to avoid the process and help me to understand that it is through the process I will be made the better. Thank you for not holding my shortcomings against me, but using my flaws to manifest your glory to me.

As I continue this journey of faith help me to rely on you more than I depend on myself. Amen.

LORD KEEP ME MOTIVATED

Notes

____

____

____

____

____

____

____

____

____

____

____

____

____

____

———————————————————————————————————————

———————————————————————————————————————

———————————————————————————————————————

———————————————————————————————————————

———————————————————————————————————————

———————————————————————————————————————

———————————————————————————————————————

———————————————————————————————————————

———————————————————————————————————————

———————————————————————————————————————

———————————————————————————————————————

———————————————————————————————————————

———————————————————————————————————————

————————

| 3 |

"Lord keep me motivated when I have to make tough decisions."

Read: Genesis 21:1-21

One of the most uncomfortable things to do is, have to make a tough decision that you know will grip your heart, once the decision is made. Like deciding whether to pull the plug on a loved one who is suffering from a medical condition and there is no other option. Or maybe it is having to decide to put a child out of your home who doesn't want to grow up and be independent. Or when you have to decide to break off a relationship that is not healthy for you.

We cannot avoid moments when we have to make tough decisions. In Genesis 21, we read about a patriarch of the faith who had a tough decision to make, as he had to decide to send away a loved one to an unknown location and never see them again. The good news is that even though we sometimes have to make tough decisions, it is ultimately God's will for these things to happen.

There are times when making a tough decision is the best option for the person it is directly affecting. What if that tough decision is the very thing that will enable that person to become what God has destined them to become? God ordains tough decisions to be made, to bring fulfillment in someone's life.

I know it may be tough but we must make the decision. During those moments, you may feel it is hard to remain faithful and motivated to God, but let this story be a source of encouragement. Nothing is ever out of place because God ordained it, even if separation is necessary.

One of the greatest lessons I learned did not come at an easy or comfortable time. I was young and immature, and all I wanted to do was play basketball, smoke illegal substances, and party. Unfortunately, everything I was doing was at the expense of someone else's finances. At that time, I worked for my mother as a van driver, picking up children in the morning, and dropping them off in the evening.

I was living the good life. I stayed at home, only paid a few bills, and had the freedom to chill out most of the day. One day I arrived at work late. I had an excuse. I accidentally overslept from partying the night before. After several talks about being more responsible, my mother had reached her point of no return, because she had enough with my excuses.

The day came when I received the call I never wanted to hear. My mother called me and said, *"You are fired, get out of my house, and find another place to stay."* I know it had to be a tough decision for her (lol) because I am her son, I depend on her, and if anything goes wrong, she would be the first person I would call. But as for me and my progression in life, being fired by my mother was the best thing for me, because it pushed me to a place where I had to be alone with God and allow him to work on me.

We are guilty of wanting to hold on to people and things so tightly that we don't allow them to grow and flourish as God has purposed for their lives. Someone may be reading the words of this page who is actually at this very point where you have to make a tough decision. The good news is that what seems to be a tough decision for you, in the mind of God, it is ordained to be so. In the text, there are some life applications to gather from the characters in the story.

Sarah reveals that sometimes we make decisions based on our emotions. (8-10)

The text says Sarah has finally given birth to Isaac, the promised son whose arrival has been long anticipated. Sarah, however, becomes irritated with Ishmael when he begins to laugh and mock the younger Isaac at his weaning party. So, Sarah, in rage, demands Abraham to cast out this slave woman Hagar and Ishmael because her son would not be an heir to the promise with her son Isaac.

We must admit that we are guilty of reacting out of emotion at times as well. There is no thought, just a reaction. The problem with reacting without thinking is it steals away our ability to consider things rationally. Sarah is in that place, demanding Abraham to throw Hagar and Ishmael out of her house. A wise woman (my wife, lol) once told me to *"Think first, react second."*

This action makes you stop and think about what you are feeling and why you are feeling the way you feel, then respond.

Abraham reveals that sometimes we must make tough decisions which are greater than we can handle. (11-13)

No decision is ever easy, but can you imagine having to put your first-born child and his mother out of your home? Abraham, after he hears Sarah's harsh demands is crushed. He is not just casting away some slave and her son, it is his child.

This incident was not the first time Abraham has had to make tough decisions. For instance, he had to decide to separate from his father's house and leave everything he knew to follow God. Abraham had to decide to separate from his nephew Lot when the herdsman began to argue. He had to decide how to handle the situation when contempt entered his home between Hagar and Sarah.

Abraham is now at another fork in the road and has a tough decision because laughter has caused Sarah to demand his son's immediate departure. Abraham is not pleased! Ismael is his son, and he has to cast him out. If you and I were in Abraham's shoes, we would also want to cry out *"Lord, keep me motivated!"*

There will be times when we must make tough decisions not based on our convictions. It may be uncomfortable, heavy on our hearts, or feel like a millstone is around our neck, but a hard decision has to be made. Here is a word of encouragement, *"Remember tough decisions are hard but necessary."*

Hagar and Ismael reveal that sometimes we are the recipients of a tough decision. (14-21)

The text tells us while Hagar and Ismael are on their new journey, they encounter a problem when they run out of water.

In desperation and exhaustion, Hagar takes her son and sits him down to die. But God has bigger plans for their lives. The text tells us that God heard the voice of the child, and he reassures Hagar of the promise he made her the first time she attempted to leave because of Sarah. In Genesis 16:9-10, God told her, *"Return to Sarah and submit to her, and I will multiply your offspring so that they cannot be numbered."*

Even though the child is at the point of death and Hagar has reached exhaustion, God confirms a principle that each of us must take hold of, which is even though it is a tough decision, we need it to reach fulfillment. God tells Hagar in Genesis 21:18, Get up, and get the boy, hold him in your hands, because it is time for you to walk into your promise.

The Bible says God opened her eyes, and she saw a well of water and gave the boy what he needed to revitalize him. The boy grew, God was with him, he became an expert in the bow, and God used his casting out in the wilderness to be the place of preparation for him to fulfill what God had destined for his life.

There will be times when we may be in the shoes of one of these characters, but be encouraged because sometimes we will have to make tough decisions that feel hard at the moment, but remember it is necessary. So, stop stressing over your tough decisions, and remember God is in control.

Prayer:

Lord, there are times when I must separate from people I love. It is in these times when I need your strength and wisdom. Lord, help me in each moment of my life not to react out of emotions but to think and reflect when I must make a tough decision. Lord, please help me to know that it is your will to bring out the best in others. Lord, if I am to be on the receiving end, allow me to realize that everything I am going through is necessary to develop me as you have purposed. Thank you for always loving me and protecting me. Amen

LORD KEEP ME MOTIVATED

Notes

| 4 |

"Lord keep me motivated when I feel the task is too big."

Lord Keep Me Motivated

Read: Genesis 6:1-22

One of the most vital roles and virtues in the Christian life is being committed to God. Unfortunately, this virtue or role is often neglected. Commitment is not just when we are in the spotlight of our peers. Commitment is that virtue that shows up when we think no one is watching.

Many in Christendom are guilty of simply being *"stage play-ers."* They look the part, but they are only acting it out. Jesus calls these types of people *"hypocrites!"* There is a danger in posing to be a committed Christian because the truth will reveal itself when life happens. When it is not authentic, we end up becoming hypocritical Christians instead.

It reminds me of a story of a young man considered for the position of Executive Vice President of a Fortune 500 company. There were discussions about his compensation, and the deliberations went long into the morning. The Board of Directors decided to adjourn for lunch and vote immediately upon their return. While in the company cafeteria, a board member stood behind the candidate as he went through the food line. He observed the candidate lift his plate and slide a piece of butter under it to avoid detection by the cashier.

When the meeting reconvened, the board member stood, shared what he had just observed, and commented, *"If we can't trust him with a three-cent piece of butter, how can we place the company in his hands?"* The candidate missed a golden opportunity because of an unguarded compromising moment. He traded a three-million-dollar compensation package for a three-cent piece of butter. Why? Because of compromise.

The question is, what about you? Have you stopped to calculate some of your losses lately? What has God promised for your life that you are not attaining because of the compromises you continue to display? God wants his children to be committed to Him, no matter what. And for us to stand up, we must stand out.

The question is, amid a world that has turned its attention and allegiance from God to itself, who does ours lie? Many have conformed to a worldly system of thought, which promotes a *"self-governing"* existence. This idea means every individual should fulfill their desires no matter the cost of relationship, morality, or ethics. We must remember two things. (1)God knows the situations surrounding us. (2) God knows our limitations.

The highlighted character in our story should remind us of ourselves because there are moments when God will call us to a task that we feel is too great for us. In those moments, if we are not careful, we lose motivation. Today, allow the example of Noah to be a source of encouragement because, like us, Noah was just a man. He was not perfect, but was willing to commit to God's instructions, even if it didn't make sense. Can you imagine the conversation between God and Noah as he asked him to build an ark?

God: Noah, I want you to build an Ark.

Noah: Lord what is an Ark?

God: Noah it is going to rain.

Noah: Lord what is rain?

God: Noah I'm going to cause a flood to happen.

Noah: Lord what do you mean by the word flood?

Although this may seem comical, we must remember that during Noah's time, there were no models of Arks to mimic. It had never rained in this magnitude, and it had never flooded. History tells us that man was becoming excessively wicked, and their hearts were away from God. Therefore, God was going to wipe out creation, but one man found favor in the eyes of the Lord, whose name was Noah.

Like Noah, we must dare to be different and stand for righteousness. We must stand for God! The wonderful thing about God is, no matter who we are or what we may do wrong, *"God knows the potential inside us even when we are not aware it exists."*

Just think, Noah built an ark because God told him to. He had no previous boat-building experience and was not a wood mason. The one characteristic that Noah possessed that all believers must strive for is a willingness to do what God says to do. No matter if we do not know how to and are uncomfortable with the idea. We must trust that God knows best.

The proverb writer gives this advice, *"Trust in the Lord with all your heart and do not lean on your own understanding but in all your ways acknowledge him and he will direct your paths." (Proverbs 3:5-6 ESV.)* [5]

This passage encourages us to know that nothing is outside God's understanding, but most things are outside ours. God makes our paths clear, but we must trust and obey his commands. God knows what purpose he can accomplish through us. We must decide to be obedient to Him. Because of Noah's willingness to do what God instructed, God granted success. God used Noah. The question is, *"Can God use you?"*

Prayer:

Lord, it is confession time. I have been guilty of questioning you when you have called me to follow you. Lord, forgive me and help me not lean on my understanding. Lord, help me to trust that you know what is best for me. And help me to avail myself to you and grant me success in all my endeavors to bring you glory. Amen.

LORD KEEP ME MOTIVATED

Notes

____

____

____

____

____

____

____

____

____

____

____

____

____

____

| 5 |

"Lord keep me motivated when I become impatient"

Lord Keep Me Motivated

Read Genesis 15:1-21

Have you ever found yourself becoming impatient? I know I have, and I believe it is because we live in a society that makes everything so convenient to the consumer that the believer has adopted this same consumer mindset with God. *"We want what we want, when we want it, and we want it now!"* Why? because we are impatient.

I have discovered when things are easy and comfortable, people become complacent. They devalue the maturation process and take for granted things will not be easy. This misunderstanding has sadly become the demise of the standards of God's people. We would rather have the ease and comfort of life, fueled by personal fulfillment and desires, without faith and obedience, which sometimes calls for unease and discomfort in our lives. As a result, we become impatient and move by our own volition, and we fail because we cannot simply wait on God.

In the text, the word *"Covenant"* is the key to understanding how God deals with his people.

A *"Covenant"* is an agreement between God and his people. This set of demands is for believers to live by, in connection to their relationship with God. The only way to live by these standards is through patience, faith, obedience, and sacrifice. Our covenant with God is not because of who we are or what we can do. It is because of what God promised, He would fulfill. We may not know when it will happen, the key is we must learn to be patient and wait on God.

Here are a few takeaways from the text:

God will give you the courage you need to wait. (1-2)

Naturally, we do not like to wait because society puts everything at our fingertips, and waiting is simply an inconvenience that we want no part of. God promised Abraham that he would defend him as he told him, *"I am your Shield!"* And he promised that he would be Abraham's exceeding reward. This promise helps the believer know:

(1) God is the *"Giver"* of all we need. (2) God is the *"Sender"* of where we are going. (3) God is the *"Provider"* of what we will need to survive. (4) God is our *"Protector"* through whatever lies ahead.

Child of God, let this be motivation and encouragement for you! Because God will be with us during those difficult times that test our patience, faith, and obedience. But we must be willing to sacrifice all to Him. The key to reaching fulfillment is to embrace the process called *"waiting."* But when we learn to wait on God with the right attitude and disposition, we know that everything he promised us he would provide. We do not need to fear! Take courage in the Lord while we wait.

The text also teaches:

God will give you the confidence you need to wait. (3-6)

Abraham's initial response to God was from a natural perspective, as he based everything on what he could see with his eyes and tangibly feel with his hands. Abraham thought it was the only way for God's promise to come true since he had no biological children. In his mind, *"Eliezer must have been the one the blessing was attached to."*

Who was Eliezer? He was his most trusted servant. If Abraham died, his eldest servant would become his heir. Therefore, without any children, Eliezer was sure to be the one God spoke of. God, however, made a *"Covenant"* with Abraham. A promise of a future realization only God could identify, understand, and manifest. Abraham desired to see and touch what he was promised before he believed. Faith says, **"Although I cannot see it, I still believe!"**

God gives Abraham the promise of his descendants being as many as the dust and stars, too numerous to count. This word from God came to Abraham when he was getting desperate over what he could not see or feel (his heir). It seemed that what God told him about his descendants was more than he could ever imagine because he had no children.

What kind of math was God doing? How can a man be the father of a great nation when he doesn't have one child yet?

But this is how God works. Abraham didn't understand *"how"* it would happen, but the text says he believed God. This promise is what God wants to give you in the face of adversity, unresolved issues, and unfulfilled dreams. We may not know *"how"* it will happen, but believe God will come through. God needs you to have confidence while you wait.

We must remember three things: (1) God is Omniscient - He knows all. (2) God is Omnipresent - He sees all. (3) God is Omnipotent - He has all power in his hands. So, when things seem impossible to comprehend, God says, *"Just wait!"* I made you a promise. You are in a covenant relationship with me, and I will fulfill what I purposed in your life. Be patient and wait on God.

God will build in you the character you need for the waiting process. (7-21)

Abraham was a man of faith, but like us, he sometimes did not demonstrate his faith with his actions. God wants to take him forward, but first, he has to build some character in him. The same is true for us as Christians. We are instructed in the Word of God to develop our relationship with Him. The believer's relationship with God is founded upon their belief in Christ's finished work on the cross. This faith is the heart-felt inner confidence that God is who He says He is and God will do what He said he will do.

Here are the actions required from us: We must be patient, faithful, obedient, and willing to sacrifice everything unto the Lord. We have already identified some of Abraham's mistakes, but thank God that when we make mistakes like Abraham, God does not stop working in us and for us.

Although human and sinful, Abraham still believed in God. We see this as Abraham asked God, *"How will I know?"* This question is not that he doesn't believe in God, it exposes there is still some faith-building necessary to be prepared for where the Lord is taking him. His question signified that he wanted a sign from God, but God gave him a sign upon the sacrifice. Notice in verse 9 that there is a specific number given. The question is, Why three years old?

God wanted all the animals to be three years old because the animals were fully grown, developed, and had maximum strength. God is to be served with our best and with maximum effort. In the Bible, cutting the animals showed Abraham the seriousness of the covenant relationship. Where are you in your faith walk? Are you impatient? Are you complaining? Have you almost given up? God says, *"Wait!"* I'm not through with you yet. I am preparing you for the next chapter of your life, but some things are required. But the key is sometimes we must learn to be patient and *"Wait"* on God.

Prayer

Dear Lord, I am guilty of being impatient. Lord, please forgive me for attempting to go around you to make things happen for myself. Lord, help me to trust in you even when I cannot physically see the miracle at work. Lord, help me to trust not in what I see but in you who made the promise. Thank you for keeping your promise and being in a covenant relationship with me. Amen.

LORD KEEP ME MOTIVATED

Notes

| 6 |

"Lord keep me motivated when my perspective is obscure."

Read: Genesis 18:1-15

What do you do when you desire something to come to pass, but it has not happened as quickly as you had hoped? How do you respond when you have been informed and promised that you will receive it but, in your estimation, the likelihood of it coming to pass seems impossible? Perspective is everything.

Everyone will find themselves at this point in their journey with God at one time or another. We have all faced a circumstance that we felt we would and should be able to handle on our own. But when that trial or storm rushes into our lives, our faith also gets swept away. Why? This *"faltering of our faith"* happens because our perspective has become clouded by human emotions. You know those times when we are feeling down, anxious, or nervous about a particular circumstance, we void out what God says and promises. The reason behind these feelings, is because we base things on what we are experiencing and forget who we are connected to.

As a believer, it is detrimental to our overall success in life and our ability to be witnesses for God to change our perspective. The Christian life is *"not"* to be lived according to human reason or understanding. This is made clear to us as we hear the words of the Proverb writer who declares that we must, *"Trust in the Lord with all your heart, and do not lean on your own understanding (Prov.3:5).* [6]

Our understanding is prohibited because we are limited in our abilities to understand beyond what we can see. The best way to describe our perspective to God's perspective is a practical scenario, for example:

Can you recall those dreaded times when you were caught in a traffic jam on the highway? You are stuck and can only see things in your immediate circumference. No matter what you do. No matter how hard you wish that you could see what the problem is ahead, the reality is you cannot.

Unfortunately, all you can do is wait until traffic clears. But God can see what is ahead and inform us of the pathway further than we can see. His view is comparable to your local News helicopter, which can see what is ahead and give you data to help you navigate and keep you informed of the pathways.

The problem with many believers is they never watch or read God's report, which he has given in 66 books. He has given us these books *"not"* as a table centerpiece. He gives us these books to help us navigate the Christian life successfully. We must stop becoming impatient, complaining, and being lackadaisical. We must learn to change our perspective as we wait.

Up until now, in the Abraham narrative, God has continued to be with Abraham amid his failures and flaws. Abraham does have some strengths, but he also has weaknesses, just as we all do. Chapter 18 shows us another dimension in the relationship-building process between God and Abraham, which reveals that we should not just sit back and recline because we still have work to do.

The Bible says some things about Abraham's encounter with these men we must observe. We will notice God revealing to Abraham both his grace and his judgment. Here are the principles the text teaches:

There is a right disposition to have while we are waiting. (1-8)

Too often, while waiting on God, we waste time doing nothing. Notice Abraham's actions when he saw the three men. The Bible says he *"ran"* and he *"bowed."* This demonstration reveals to us that he moved with urgency.

This should teach us a valuable lesson. While we are waiting on God's promise to come to pass, we should always be aware of his presence and never sit idle. We should follow the example of Abraham and get to work diligently, and also get those connected to us, working for the cause as well.

Today the family structure has taken strides backwards. It is alarming that parents can come to the place where God is and leave their children at home and not have them join in serving the Lord! We must begin to encourage them and put them to work as well. This word *"quick"* should imply to us that there is an urgency that is needed in every believer's life to work for the Lord.

There is a wrong disposition to have while you're waiting. (9-15)

If there is a correct way to do something, there is also a wrong way. Here we will focus on Sarah's disposition. The text says, Sarah was questioned about listening in on the conversation, she laughed to herself in disbelief. Sarah's actions were a sign of having the wrong disposition, because *"she laughed."*

But why would she laugh? Maybe it is because she begins to reason within herself about her inabilities. Maybe she begins to doubt the possibility of her husband's abilities. Sarah demonstrates what a wrong disposition is when you are wrong and you know it.

If we will be honest, there are times when we too have responded more like Sarah than Abraham. We also look at the impossibilities within ourselves and do not stop to consider God's words to Sarah, *"Is there anything too hard for God?"* God always keeps his promise, and we must hold to our faith in Him, even when we cannot see what God is doing.

Prayer:

Lord, there are times when I am guilty of wanting to know what's next, and I grow impatient because I am not seeing life from your perspective. Please forgive me and help me to trust your word when I cannot identify how you are working the details out in my life. Lord, change my disposition and help me learn to wait on you and work for you while I wait. Thank you for the victory that you have already promised me, and help me to rely on you. Amen.

LORD KEEP ME MOTIVATED

Notes

____

____

____

____

____

____

____

____

____

____

____

____

____

____

| 7 |

"Lord keep me motivated when I have allowed my outward sins to bring inward shame."

Read Psalm 51:1-19

The late novelist Alex Haley kept a picture in his office of a turtle sitting on a fence. Often, he would be asked about the meaning of the picture, and he would explain: *"If you see a turtle sitting on a fence you know it didn't get there by itself."* And that is the facts of life, each of us must come to acknowledge. We are not self -made, and we are not self-sufficient.

Our total existence is founded upon God's grace, and mercy alone. When there is a failure to remember this, our actions will become distasteful, disrespectful and disgraceful. We will treat people without dignity. We will lie, steal, and cheat just to get ahead. And what is even sadder is we will lie to ourselves that what we are doing is right. As a result, we will find ourselves in the much-needed state of the author of this Psalm, needing to repent and plead for God's mercy.

David, the writer of the Psalm had an outward confession of an inward disgrace. David, through his cry out to God shows us what true repentance is. The word *"Repentance"* means to have a change of mind and begin to go in a different direction. This Psalm is connected to one of the most difficult times in David's life when as a result of his actions, his child was taken away from him in death. **(Read 2 Samuel 11 and 12)**

After hearing the error of his ways David cries out, **"Have mercy on me, O God!"** And this is where true repentance takes shape in our lives as well. We must see ourselves for who we really are.

Like David we must have:

A remorse for the sin we have committed against God. (1-2)

David has reached the place of *"Remorse"* for the sins he has committed. Therefore, he asked the Lord to blot out his transgressions. What David is saying, don't just void out my transgressions but wash me and cleanse me of any trace of it. I believe from personal experience, this is a place where people struggle with being motivated. There is a need to make sure we pause in our prayers, and ask God simply for Mercy.

Why is this so important? Because too often we can get on our knees and confess our sins but no sooner than we arise from our knees, we forget, and never have a change of mindset or direction. Maybe that is where you are today? And please do not feel like you are all alone, because I was guilty of what I call, *"kind-of-fessing"* instead of genuinely confessing my sins to God. And without true confession there is no true repentance. The text also teaches us we must take responsibility for the sins we have committed.

We must also take responsibility for the sins we commit. (3-4)

David in the Psalm expresses the statement *"Lord Have mercy on me,"* as he realizes the affects his sins has brought in his life. In 2 Samuel 11, David commits the unthinkable when he impregnated a married woman named Bathsheba. David, in a failed attempt to cover up the incident had her husband Uriah killed. Due to the wickedness of his actions, he was informed by Nathan the prophet, God was not pleased. David discovered, although the act was with Bathsheba and to Uriah, his transgression was against the Lord.

After hearing the news from Nathan, David now takes responsibility for his sins, when he says *"I know my transgressions and my sin is ever before me."* In other words, *"I know what I have done."* David was not coming to God blaming other people for why he was in the situation he was in. He went to God knowing he was guilty and the results that followed were justified.

How about you, do you take responsibility for your sins? I know we think when we hurt, talk about and backbite others it really doesn't matter, but David shows us when we act unrighteous toward others, it does matter because it is sin against God. That is why David says *"against you and you only have I sinned and have done evil in your sight."*

There is nothing you can do and no place you can go where God isn't. So, when we think what we are doing is okay, we should stop and consider this truth; *"Everything we do, God sees and knows."* The problem is that when we don't confess our sins with a heart of true repentance, we will continue to justify our ungodly actions. That is why people continue to live unholy when God has called us to be holy.

There must also be a realization of the sins we've committed. (5-7)

David realizes that sin has invaded his being and knows the only way to be delivered is for a transformation on the inside! He says, *"I was brought forth in iniquity and in sin, my mother conceived me."* This is what we need to be aware of, we sin not because of the act, but because we are born in sin.

The only way to be free from sin is to have a transformed life by the power of God. God does not change outside in; he changes us inside out. David says, *"Lord, you delight in the truth in the inward being, and you teach in the secret heart."* If you want your actions to be holy, your life to be focused, and to live a life that pleases God, there must be a change on the inside.

David's words through this Psalm are a plea to God to create a clean heart, restore the joy of his salvation, and deliver him from guilt. David understands a principle we all need to understand, *"When God cleans us up, we can be effective in teaching others about who He is."*

Prayer:

Lord, today I come confessing I have sinned against you. I have allowed sin and self to take my focus off of you. So, today I repent of all my sins and ask you for your mercy. Thank you Lord, for not holding against me every flaw and failure I have. And thank you for the shed blood of Jesus on the cross, who has justified me by my faith in him. Help me to change my ways and my heart in order to please you in all I do. Amen

LORD KEEP ME MOTIVATED

Notes

____

____

____

____

____

____

____

____

____

____

____

____

____

____

____

____

| 8 |

"Lord keep me motivated when I feel I can't go on any further."

Read: Mark 5:25-34

Sickness is one of the great interrupters of life. It enters without knocking, stopping all plans, mocking one's certainties, and diminishing ones hope for the future. So, the question is, How can you push when life seems to have you in a stuck position? What do you do when life sends an interruption in your path, and you feel as if you aren't able to go on any further?

Lance Armstrong is a living testimony, and inspiration for all facing some interruptions. In July of 2001, Armstrong made the headlines for winning his third Tour De France, just five years after receiving the devastating news of being diagnosed with an advance stage of testicular cancer. Can you imagine the devastation that news brought him? No longer would he be able to do what he loved! His lifestyle, would be altered forever!

How could he make it through his interruptions? Lance says some words to encourage our hearts. He says, *"We all have unrealized capabilities that will only emerge in our crisis. We have capabilities for enduring, living, hope, caring and enjoying. Each time we overcome pain, we grow. Cancer was not my breaking it was my making!"* Lance's words are motivating because just as he faced his crisis, he became more compassionate, complete, and intelligent about God and more alive.

In Mark 5, we see Jesus's fame has spread rapidly. People have heard about him healing the sick, raising the dead and giving sight to the blind. Jesus is a picture of hope to all in need. As Jesus is on his journey, he's asked to come and heal the daughter of a man named Jairus, whose daughter is dying. But, while Jesus is on his way to perform a miracle, His walk is interrupted by a very sick woman with an immediate need! Her face marked with lines of agony. Her body is racking with pain.

Who is this woman? We do not know her name. We do not know where she came from. And we are not told who her people were. All we know is she was a woman in agony. For twelve long agonizing years she had suffered with the same issue. She wants relief. She wants restoration. She wants health. She wants a normal life, and hopes Jesus can heal and help her with the issue. The woman teaches how to move when we feel like we cannot go further. Allow her story to be motivation for you even when a crisis arises in your life.

The woman pushed pass her despair. (25-26)

Have you ever had an issue in your life that has caused you to feel out of control? Certainly this is the feeling this woman had. She has lost all sense of identity. She feels uncertain about life. She is an outcast and has emptied herself of all her resources. Now she feels hopeless, until she hears about a man named Jesus.

This woman does not sit still in her condition, but keeps pushing forward in hope of her healing. The same holds true for you. Do not allow your pain or distress to cause you to sit still. Keep on pushing towards Jesus, who is able to give you everything you need.

The woman pushed towards the master in her desperation. (27-28)

This woman was desperate, and willing to try anything to bring healing to her body. She had heard about Jesus being a healer. Strangely, something awakens, and resolution gradually builds in her heart. Her actions demonstrate an urge to seek Jesus.

Can you imagine the conversation she is having within herself? She may have asked, *"Should I touch Him? Yes, I will. It wouldn't hurt just to touch Him, right? But where should I touch him? Maybe on the head? No, that would be irreverent! Maybe on the hand? No, that would be too familiar! Maybe his robe! Certainly there cannot be any harm in touching His robe as He passes. Okay, it is settled when he pass by, I believe it would be enough just to touch the hem of His robe.*

Her resolve was definite, if I just touch the hem of Him, I will be made well. This woman knows in her heart Jesus can heal, or at least she is desperate enough to try. She squeezes through the crowd and reaches out to touch His garment and while others are bumping into Jesus casually, she reaches out and touches Him intentionally.

What does this say to us? When we have done all we could possibly do for ourselves, and we find our situation getting worse instead of getting better, what is left to do? The text teaches us to do what this desperate woman did. We must get past our feelings. We must stop trying to reason within ourselves. We must know there is hope because Jesus is available. Push through your crowds of despair and discouragement, and reach out to the Master for everything you need.

The woman pushed and reached out for her deliverance. (29-34)

As instantaneously as the women touched Jesus, He sensed healing power had gone out of Him. No one else noticed her, but the person who she needed did. She had been a daughter of death, but now she has become a daughter of life. In an instant, her body regains control, is granted a new identity, has a certain future, regains her place in society, and discovers hope. In an instant, Jesus heals her sickness, eases her suffering, grants her freedom, and saves her soul.

And that is what he can give someone today, an instantaneous change. Life will have difficulties, and we will feel we cannot go on any further. Let this woman's faith serve as an example that God can keep you motivated, but we must begin to reach out to Him.

Prayer:

Lord, help me when I attempt to do things on my own, and remember I cannot do anything without you. Thank you for being strength in weakness, courage in moments of fear, and hope in my anxieties. Help me to trust you more and stop trying to depend on myself to handle what only you can. Amen.

LORD KEEP ME MOTIVATED

Notes

____

____

____

____

____

____

____

____

____

____

____

____

____

____

____

| 9 |

"Lord keep me motivated when I am hurt by people I love."

Read: Genesis 37:1-6

The most devastating emotion one can experience is feeling hated, hurt, and harassed by family members. Unlike friends, there is a higher degree of agony. Nothing is worse than feeling hurt by those we love. And when it happens, it can cause us to lose motivation.

Some family hardships are inherited, while others are self-inflicted, but the good news is no matter what end of the spectrum you have been on, God can change that situation around for you. There are many who are hurt daily by family members. Unfortunately, this hurt does not leave but, it does not have to control or consume you. There is a danger in holding on to hurt caused by family because of hate and animosity which can build up. It will cause a person not to be able to move forward into the purpose God has for their lives.

Joseph, who goes through a series of hardships in his life, teaches us a valuable lesson: "*As long as God is on our side, we don't have to act, speak, or respond to life's hardships like everyone else.*"

We can continue to stay motivated when we demonstrate what the Psalmist declares, *"Be still and know"* that God is on our side. After Joseph had gone through these hardships, he understood God had used every painful experience to prepare him for his future.

Here is a brief highlight of his story:

- Joseph was despised by his brothers, *but* Loved by his father.
- Joseph was Hated for his words *but* was Honored with Visions.
- Joseph was cast into a Pit *but* there was no water in it.
- Joseph was Sold as a slave *but* God put him in the right hands.

The key to making it through the hardships, the heartbreaks, the headaches, and the hate demonstrated by family members is to understand when we are faithful to God, he interjects a divine *"But"* in our situation, which changes the scope of what we are facing.

Maybe you have been despised by your family. You don't have to allow what they have said or done to make you feel less than who God has made you to be. You can soar to higher heights. You can have ultimate success. And you will be blessed. Just remind yourself, *"But"* God!

Maybe you are being hated by your family, and it seems as if they want to destroy your confidence, remind yourself, *"But"* God!

Maybe you have been cast into some pits, and your family is the reason why you are there! Remind yourself, although they threw me into the pit *"But"* God made sure that what they have done, will not hurt, bury, or destroy me.

And finally, even if you have been despised, hated, cast into a pit, or sold as a slave, remember that you are not what they call you. **"You are in the Master's hands."** And in his hands, there is hope, joy, peace, love, and safety. God can heal our broken hearts! We need to take Joseph's words and make them our own, *"What you meant for evil, God meant it for my good!"*

Prayer:

Lord, there have been times when I have been hurt by those I love most. Help me not to harbor hate in my heart, and help me bridle my tongue less I say or do something that will not bring glory to your name. Lord, help me to understand every experience I am facing is purposeful. Keep me drawing near to you and remind me that you are always on my side. Amen.

LORD KEEP ME MOTIVATED

Notes

____

____

____

____

____

____

____

____

____

____

____

____

____

____

____

| 10 |

"Lord keep me motivated when life just happens"

Read: 2 Kings 4:1-7

In the comical movie *"Life,"* Ray and Claude are two men serving a *"Life"* sentence. The irony of their story is that it depicts the uncertainties of life at its finest. For 60 years, they witnessed hardship and kindness, cruelty and forgiveness, life and death. Neither man was innocent because they were both guilty of having character flaws.

Claude covered his gambling flaw well with his education, potential wife, and new job. While Ray is a loud-mouth, loud-acting, smooth-talking hustler, and unlike Claude, he does not hide who he is. Although these men were different, they experienced the same reality many of us experienced. No matter who we are and how we try to dress or cover up, *"Life"* has a way of happening to us whether we like it or not.

But here is the good news and an important fact that every child of God needs to know and understand. God is the provider of all you need amid *"Life's Hardships!"* When life happens, many forget this fact, most times unknowingly. Why? Because people allow how things appear to drive them into desperation, anxiety, depression, and misery.

For example, have you ever been praying to God about that failing marriage, disrespectful spouse, disobedient children, that dead-end job, the devastating loss of a loved one, or a disheartening message from the doctor's office, and nothing changes instantly? Things seem to be getting worse rather than getting better. Life has a way of making us feel as if it is not one thing it is another.

What do you do when those times of uncertainty arise in your life? Many will become angry, others will become irritated, and some will become depressed. There are times when we have felt that all hope is gone. As a result, our faith begins to falter, dreams diminish, and our obedience to God's will becomes an obstacle.

In the text, there is a story of the widow of one of the sons of the prophets. This woman pictures the same feelings we feel at one time or another. We have all felt helpless and hopeless. This widow's story illustrates how God's infinite grace and power can supply all our needs. God can take a person who is a victim of debt, desperation, depression, and distress and fill them with joy, richness, and liberty.

The great news is God has already provided you with what you need. The problem is sometimes we do not realize the value of what we have already received from him. Maybe you have an issue you have been praying to God about and it seems like all hope is gone. Let this text encourage you, God has already given you what you need.

If we are going to make it through the hardships of life, we must learn to do a few things, demonstrated by the widow in the text: (1) We must dismiss all of our fears. (2) We must demonstrate faithfulness to God's instructions. (3) We must depend on God's provisions. Tough times will come, but we can make it knowing God will prepare us with what we need, protect us from what we don't need, and provide for us *"how to"* use what we need.

Prayer:

Lord, I am guilty of allowing moments when life happens to make me nervous and anxious about how I will make it through. Lord, forgive me for relying on my strength when you have provided me with what I needed most. Help me in those moments to remember all that you have already given me because you gave me your Son and the Holy Spirit, to comfort me in times of weakness. Thank you for always loving and keeping me even when I do not deserve it. Amen

LORD KEEP ME MOTIVATED

Notes

References

1. Romans 6:1-2 ESV
2. Colossians 1:28-29. ESV
3. Johnson, Barbara. *Boomerang Joy: Joy That Goes around, Comes around: 60 Devotions.* Walker & Company, 2000.
4. Matthew 6:25. ESV
5. Chicago Mass Choir, 2005
6. Proverbs 3:5-6. ESV
7. Proverbs 3:5. ESV

LORD KEEP ME MOTIVATED

ABOUT THE AUTHOR

Personal testimony:

My personal story may be similar to some but will be uncommon with most. I grew up in a Christian home. My father was a minister, who also was a preacher's kid. I was a fifth-generation preacher's kid whom the Lord also called to become a preacher and pastor.

Growing up there was a constant pull for ministry and church attendance. I remember going to BTU, Saturday Bible class, and Sunday School, hearing about Jesus and learning about the Bible. While being in close proximity to God is different than being in a relationship with him. I would later realize that I was guilty of only being in close proximity and did not have a relationship with Him.

Every second Saturday of the month, we would go out and witness to the neighborhood, knocking on doors and asking people the questions, "Do you know Jesus? And if you died today, where would you spend eternity?" Even as a child, I believed these were heavy questions to start a conversation with. In many cases, I witnessed the dread on people's faces. Were these tactics working? Was it a great way to connect people to Christ?

I recognized old methods of outreach were not effective. God was calling for something different. He called me to share Him differently, biblically, and impactfully. That is when Connect Ministries launched, and my journey as an author began.

LORD KEEP ME MOTIVATED